THE GIRL WHO COLLECTED HER OWN ECHO

The Girl Who Collected Her Own Echo is a therapeutic story about finding friendship. In the story, a little girl lives by herself and loves to sing. One day whilst she is singing in a mysterious cave, she thinks that her echo must be the sound of other children singing, but she is too shy to approach them. When she meets a boy who loved hearing her sing but was too shy to approach her, she realises that they were both lonely and they can sing together as friends. This beautifully illustrated storybook will appeal to all children, and can be used by practitioners, educators and parents as a tool to discuss friendship and feelings of loneliness.

Juliette Ttofa is a Specialist Senior Educational Psychologist with 15 years' experience working with children and young people. She specialises in supporting resilience and well-being in vulnerable children.

Julia Gallego is a picture book illustrator and designer, and a graduate of the Manchester School of Art.

For my friends
X

First published 2018 by Routledge
2 Park Square, Milton Park, Abingdon, Oxon OX14 4RN

52 Vanderbilt Avenue, New York, NY 10017

Routledge is an imprint of the Taylor & Francis Group, an informa business

British Library Cataloguing-in-Publication Data
A catalogue record for this book is available from the British Library

Library of Congress Cataloging-in-Publication Data
A catalog record for this book has been requested

ISBN: 978-1-138-30889-3 (pbk)
ISBN: 978-1-315-14320-0 (ebk)

Typeset in Calibri
by Apex CoVantage, LLC

The Girl Who Collected Her Own Echo

A Story About Friendship

By Juliette Ttofa

Illustrated by Julia Gallego

Routledge
Taylor & Francis Group

LONDON AND NEW YORK

There was once a very lonely, very frightened girl.
She lived alone except for a nameless cat...

She lived in a wooden hut on her own,
on an island surrounded by the sea.

The little girl did not have many possessions.

She didn't have any friends. She didn't have a family.

Her only company apart from her cat, were the birds in the trees, the fish in the lake and the goat on the mountain side.

But she did have a single piece of chalk and she loved to draw.

She used the chalk to draw out games like hopscotch on the ground.

Because she was lonely, she would also draw people.

She drew a Mummy to lie with on the floor at night.

She drew a teddy bear to cuddle while she slept.

And outside her hut, she drew a friend with curly hair and kind eyes to play with.

The little girl also loved to sing.

Every day, she would sing to her chalk family.

And, as she drew more and more friends on the ground outside her hut, she would sing more and more songs.

Her songs were so sad, yet so full of beauty, that they attracted many animals from all over the island, who would become enchanted by the melancholy music and try to grasp the air as if it was filled with magic.

The little girl sang with all her heart, hoping that one day a real person would hear her song and find her.

3

Then one winter's day, as she was collecting sticks for the fire, she came across a cave.

It was a very special grotto filled with sparkling stalactites which dripped like jewels from the roof.

Either side of the cave were small hollows filled with pools of water. She imagined the hollows were tiny little worlds, in which tiny little people lived.

So, the little girl began to draw chalk people on the walls of the cave.

And as she drew, she sang her sweet, captivating songs.

Each day she would go back to the cave and draw more and more people on the walls until she had ventured quite far inside.

But one day, as she was singing deep inside the cave, another girl's voice came singing back to her.

The little girl was so surprised and so scared that she ran and ran all the way home.

But the next day she was curious, so she went further into the cave. She began to sing, and sure enough the same thing happened again.

"There *are* other children living in this cave!" she thought. "They are singing my songs back to me!"

This time the little girl was feeling a bit braver so she stayed a bit longer.

"Hello?" she called.

"Hello?" came the reply.

Frightened, she rushed back to the safety of her home.

6

The following day, the girl had an idea.

To stop herself from feeling so lonely she would go to the cave with a flask and collect the sound of the cave children's voices!

For she was too scared to go really deep inside the cave to meet the real children who were singing back to her.

So early the next morning she skipped down to the cave with her flask.

She crept into the middle of the cave, sang into the gaping cavern and waited for another child to sing back.

Then, when the voice came back, the little girl quickly opened her flask, scooped up the song and shut the lid tightly again.

She took the flask home, labelled it and put it neatly onto her kitchen shelf.

The little girl repeated this, day in day out, for seven days, each time singing a new song, until she had run out of flasks and containers to use.

While the flasks gave her some companionship, she dared not open them in case she lost the sound of the song.

And she daren't go further into the cave to meet the cave children.

So she remained as alone as before.

And she carried on drawing people with her chalk.

And singing her beautiful, beguiling songs.

Until one day, her cat was chasing a mouse in the kitchen, and, as he climbed up onto the shelves, he accidentally knocked off a flask.

It fell to the ground with a clatter, and as it finally came to rest on the wooden floor, its lid popped open.

The little girl rushed over to stifle the song and stuff it quickly back into the flask.
She held the flask to her ear like a shell, listening for a sound.
But, no sound came out – no song escaped – the flask seemed to be empty.

She shook the empty flask upside down in shock.

"Who has stolen the song in my flask?" cried the little girl, "I must keep guard over my flasks tonight!"

So the little girl sat all night in a little rocking chair by the fire in the kitchen and tried to keep watch.

She fell asleep, and as she slept, gentle snow fell on the ground outside, covering all her chalk people with a glistening cloak of white.

The little girl awoke the next morning and had not noticed a thing all night.

However, when she checked the flasks the next morning – they were all empty! All the songs had been taken.

"My songs have all gone!" she cried.

Sad and disappointed the little girl collapsed onto the floor, enveloped by the chalk Mummy she had drawn.

She had lost all of her friends' songs and she felt very, very lonely.

It was only then that she spotted something down on the ground...

It was a tiny trickle of water.

She followed the trail of melted snow to the door of her little hut and as she opened the door she gasped as she noticed footprints in the newly fallen snow.

She followed the footprints all the way down the mountain, past the lake, through the trees, past the cave and to a sandy beach.

There she noticed something she had never seen before – a small, make-shift den.

The little girl tip-toed tentatively inside the den and then she caught sight of it: a giant cooking pot with a huge lid.

The little girl was a bit worried – for she had read fairy stories where big cooking pots are used for boiling small animals and small children!

But something seemed to be calling her and she couldn't resist peering inside the pot. So she stepped nearer and nearer, and went to lift the lid...

But before she could open it, a small boy with curly hair and kind eyes appeared in the doorway and they both let out a scream!

"You! Are you my song thief?" cried the little girl. "Give me my songs back!" she demanded.

The boy froze to the spot, and spoke not a word.

Instead, he moved slowly towards the pot and lifted the lid.

14

Suddenly, the most melodic music flew out of the pot.
A symphony of songs spun and woven together in perfect harmony.

"The cave children's songs!" cried the little girl in happiness. "You have made them into a chorus!"

Then the boy spoke:

"There are no cave children – these songs are only the memory of sound; the whispering echoes of your own voice," he confessed.

"I heard you singing one day and followed the mysterious sound as it drifted in the air. It was so good to hear another person's voice that I followed you back to your house and stole one of your flasks while you slept. But the songs were so beautiful that I could not stop stealing them to make even lovelier music."

16

The little girl looked angry but the boy went on:

"I'm sorry I stole them from you, they belong to you. But you see, I have been so lonely and scared since I arrived on this island. Your songs made me feel less alone. And I was too nervous to come and say hello."

The little girl's jaw dropped open in disbelief.

And then she began to smile.

She had been collecting her own echo because she was lonely.

And now, a strange, yet familiar boy had stolen her echo because he was lonely too.

And, all the time, neither one of them had said a word to each other.

The pot was empty now. And there were no more flasks left. But the girl knew just what to do.

She started to sing.

And this time, her friend sang with her.